# SURVIVING THE MONEY JUNGLE

A Junior High Study in
Handling Money

Larry Burkett

Focus on the Family Publishing
Pomona, California 91799

**Surviving the Money Jungle**
© 1990 by Larry Burkett

Revised from *God's Guide Through the Money Jungle* by Larry Burkett. Copyright © 1985 by Christian Financial Concepts.

Scripture quotations, unless otherwise noted, are from *The Holy Bible, New International Version.* Copyright © 1973, 1978, 1984 by International Bible Society. All rights reserved. Used with permission of Zondervan Bible Publishers.

Other versions used:
(NASB) *The New American Standard Bible.* Copyright © 1975 by the Lockman Foundation. Used by Permission.

(TEV) *Today's English Version: Good News for Modern Man.* Copyright © 1966, 1971, 1976 by the American Bible Society. Used by Permission.

First printing, 1990
Printed in the United States of America

**Larry Burkett, Surviving the Money Jungle**
**Summary:** A course for junior high young people on managing personal finances according to biblical principles.

ISBN 0-929608-77-1

**Focus on the Family Publishing**
Rolf Zettersten, Vice President
Dean Merrill, Vice President, Communications
Wes Haystead, Curriculum Editor
Dave and Neta Jackson, Contributing Editors
Cover Illustration, Clint Hansen
Illustrations, Bruce Day
Design, Jerry Price

Pomona, CA 91799

# CONTENTS

**Introduction**

**Lessons:**

# INTRODUCTION

If you're like other kids your age, money is becoming more important to you than ever. You may still receive an allowance, and you may be earning money at odd jobs—baby sitting, yard work, etc.—or you may have a regular, part-time job.

Whatever your case, you probably want to learn the best way of spending that hard-to-come-by cash.

The following are highlights from some of the lessons in this course. If even a few interest you, this course is for you. If for some reason you're not interested in money at all, then you might still want to know why everyone else is.

- In Lesson 3 you'll find out the most satisfying attitude toward work when you discover that God is your real Boss.
- Lesson 4 takes a good look at all the things you may think you own.
- How much money would it take to really satisfy you? Discover "The Secret of Contentment," in Lesson 5.
- Do you ever struggle with honesty in handling money? Lesson 8 will help you understand why God lets you face such temptations.
- Have you ever heard someone say, 'You can't take it with you'—referring to what happens to your money when you die? Well, the Bible tells how to send your treasure on ahead to be deposited in the 'bank' of heaven so you can enjoy it after you die. Find out how in Lesson 9.
- Suppose a panhandler approaches you on the street and asks for a quarter. Should you give away some of your hard-earned money? Lesson 12 has some thoughtful suggestions for "Who Deserves Help."

The lessons of this course are designed to be done in class as a group study course. Or, you may want to go through it at home, asking your parents to work along with you. If you should choose to do that, you will need one Teacher's Guide for your family and this Student Workbook for yourself. Even if you are part of a group study, it will be helpful to review each session with your parents.

*Surviving the Money Jungle* is not the final authority on what God has to say to young people about money, but it is a good starting place that shows that the Bible has a lot of good advice for handling money.

# THIS WAY TO FREEDOM

**In this lesson, you will...**
- **Learn some of the causes and symptoms of financial bondage;**

- **Discover that God desires His people to escape those problems and find financial freedom.**

## STEP 1
## *Some Things About Money Bug Me!*

Do some things about money bug you? Well, don't worry! You're not alone. Look at the list below and put a check by whichever statements are true in your life.

- ☐ 1. I worry about having enough money for summer camp, school clothes, new bike, etc.
- ☐ 2. I feel like I never have enough money.
- ☐ 3. I'm lost when it comes to planning a budget.
- ☐ 4. I hate to spend my own money. I'd rather get money from my parents.
- ☐ 5. When I go into a store, I always end up buying something. I can't "just look."
- ☐ 6. I wish I didn't have to have a job.
- ☐ 7. I'm bugged because I don't have as many nice things as my friends have.
- ☐ 8. I always owe my parents or friends money. I guess I just forget to pay them back.
- ☐ 9. It always seems like I'm the one who has money and my friends never do. They always ask me to loan them a few dollars. I wish they'd use their own money.
- ☐ 10. I usually have more money than my friends. I guess I like how that makes me feel.

## STEP 2
# *Symptoms of Being Trapped by Money*

How can you tell if you're trapped in a money problem? The Bible gives us some pretty reliable symptoms of money trouble. For example, "No desire to earn money" is a sure sign of trouble, according to 2 Thessalonians 3:10. (It says if a person doesn't work, he or she shouldn't be able to eat.)

1. Match the following symptoms of money trouble with the scriptures that talk about them. Be careful! You might have to think while you read.

   | | |
   |---|---|
   | • Dishonesty | Ecclesiastes 2:10,11 |
   | • Not giving to God's work | Proverbs 3:9,10 |
   | • Too many risks, hasty decisions | Proverbs 28:20 |
   | • Overdue debts | Ephesians 5:5 |
   | • Hoarding | Proverbs 28:6 |
   | • Worry about future needs | Matthew 6:25 |
   | • Jealousy of what others have | 2 Thessalonians 3:10 |
   | • No desire to earn money | Matthew 6:19,20 |
   | • Wasting | Psalm 37:21 |

2. Pick two or three symptoms from the list and write a description of a situation you have seen happen which illustrates that particular symptom. It might be something that happened to you, a friend, or an adult.

   Here's a sample description of the symptom from 2 Thessalonians:

   **Symptom:** No desire to earn money.
   **Description:** Our youth group worked to raise money for summer camp. Kevin never did anything. Our leader told him he wouldn't get any of the money we raised. Kevin said, "Who wants to go to camp, anyway?" I'm not sure if Kevin really wasn't interested in camp or just didn't want to work.

   Symptom: _____
   Description: _____
   _____

   Symptom: _____
   Description: _____
   _____

   Symptom: _____
   Description: _____
   _____

## STEP 3
## *Diagnosing the Problem*

Everyone knows that a symptom is not the cause of trouble. The Bible helps us know what the deeper problems are that can cause a person to struggle with money.

1. Begin at START and follow the path. At each fork in the road, look up and read the Bible verse describing an inner problem which leads to trouble with money—and everything else. At least one route from each intersection is a problem which will lead you into a money trap. Only one path will take you to real success.

2. Now, go through the following symptoms of financial bondage. (In Step 2 you have already looked up the verses for them.) Under each symptom fill in what you think might be the underlying, inner problem(s) causing that symptom. (You can select problems from The Deeper Problems maze. See the two examples below.) Not everyone will have the same answers, and you may list more than one problem under each symptom.

Symptom: Overdue debts (Psalm 37:21).
Problem(s): Ignorance, selfishness, greed

Symptom: Not giving to God's work (Proverbs 3:9,10).
Problem(s): Disobedience, no spiritual commitment, putting money first, greed

Symptom: Dishonesty (Proverbs 28:6).
Problem(s): _____

_____

Symptom: Too many risks, hasty decisions (Proverbs 28:20).
Problem(s): _____ greed, get rich ke

Symptom: Wasting (Ecclesiastes 2:10,11).
Problem(s): _____ laziness, greed pride

Symptom: Hoarding (Matthew 6:19,20).
Problem(s): _____ Ignorance
lack of spiritual commit

Symptom: Worry about future needs (Matthew 6:25).
Problem(s): _____ selfish _____ putting wrong things first

Symptom: Jealous of what others have (Ephesians 5:5).
Problem(s): _____ put wrong first

Symptom: No desire to earn money (2 Thessalonians 3:10).
Problem(s): _____ laziest
selfishness finacell ingerance

## STEP 4
## *The Road to Financial Freedom*

"Whoever loves money never has money enough;
whoever loves wealth is <u>never satisfied</u> with his income.
This too is meaningless." (Ecclesiastes 5:10)

**1.** What do you think this verse means? *take heed.*

_____

_____

"But remember the LORD your God,
for it is <u>he who gives you the ability to produce wealth</u>,
and so confirms his covenant." (Deuteronomy 8:18)

**2.** And what do you think this verse means? *don't rely on yourself but on God because its up to him MATT 6:33*

_____

**3.** Do you think every Christian should have lots of material possessions? Why or why not? *yes because I'm one of them. No actually because the less you have the more you have to rely on God.*

**Think:** Has God promised luxury to His children? Or has He promised to meet our needs? Do His promises of wealth refer to money or to inner qualities like peace and joy? If you're still not sure, read Philippians 4:19 and 1 Timothy 6:17.

**4.** What are one or two things you would like to learn about managing your money during this course?_____

_____

_____

_____

# GOODBYE, MONEY WORRIES!

**In this lesson, you will . . .**
- Discover how God builds our trust in Him to provide for our needs;
- Identify your personal money worries;
- Extend your trust in God's provision.

## STEP 1
## *I Sometimes Worry*

1. Complete this statement: I wish I could afford (be specific) because

2. What things might people do because they are worried about not having enough money?

3. Do you trust God to provide your needs?
   ☐ Always?  ☑ Sometimes?  ☐ Not Sure?  ☐ Hardly Ever?  ☐ Never?

   Or, do you rely on your own efforts?
   ☐ Always?  ☑ Sometimes?  ☐ Not Sure?  ☐ Hardly Ever?  ☐ Never?

   Or, maybe you count on your parents?
   ☐ Always?  ☐ Sometimes?  ☐ Not Sure?  ☑ Hardly Ever?  ☐ Never?

   Perhaps you think you don't have much opportunity to choose between trusting God's provision and trusting your own efforts, but you really do. You probably make many more financial decisions than you think you do.

   Now is a good time to begin learning to trust God to provide for you. And, hopefully, when you've completed this Bible study, you'll be well on your way!

## STEP 2
### *God's Answers to Money Worries*

**Read Matthew 6:25-34 to see what Jesus said about worry.** (He didn't mention money, but He did talk about important things we buy with money.)

1. In your own words, what does Jesus say we are to do instead of worrying about money and the things it can buy?

_____

_____

_____

_____

2. Would living by Matthew 6:33 lead to laziness? Why or why not?

_____

_____

_____

"But seek first his kingdom and his righteousness, and all these things will be given to you as well" (Matthew 6:33).

## STEP 3
### *How God Builds Our Trust*

Why is it hard to trust God? Maybe we lack confidence in God's love. Or, maybe we lack confidence in His power. If we don't believe God cares about our needs, we'll naturally trust our own efforts more than we'll trust God's promises.

Trust doesn't grow in a vacuum. You learn to trust someone because he proves himself trustworthy. God understands that. He longs to demonstrate His trustworthiness to all His children.

## A story about trust...

Imagine that one day a man knocks on your door. When you answer, he says, "I'm going to give you $50 in two weeks." He then leaves you his card and shuts the door.

You think, "How strange that was." Then you start checking him out. You begin to talk to people who might know something about him.

You discover that he is a multi-billionaire and that he has given thousands of dollars to people. Knowing this, your confidence in him grows. But, still, you don't have any real trust in him because he hasn't given you any money.

However, in two weeks he returns and delivers the $50. Your trust in him suddenly grows.

Then, he says, "I've decided to give you $1,000 in two more weeks."

You already know that he is a multi-billionaire, so you know he has the resources, and he has already given you $50. But $1,000 is so much more. Why would anyone give away that much? Then, in talking to other people, you discover that this man has occasionally given away that much in the past. You also discover something else: Everyone who knows him says that he has never lied—no matter what. When he says that he's going to do something, he always does it.

In two weeks, he returns and hands you the $1,000. Now your trust really grows. Over the next few months, he continues to give you more and more money! Each time your trust in him grows.

Then one day he comes to you after being away for some time and says, "In three months I will give you $100,000."

Well, by this time you have absolute confidence in him. You know exactly how he operates. You know that he has the funds, and you know that once he says something, it will be done. You also learn that he has given hundreds of thousands of dollars to other people as well. And so, with full confidence, you can plan how you are going to spend that money, knowing he's going to deliver exactly what he promises.

Compare the story of the generous multi-billionaire with what the Bible tells about your Heavenly Father.

**1.** Why can we trust God? _____

_____

_____

**2.** Why then do many people not trust God? _____

_____

_____

**3.** What's the first step in trusting God? _____

_____

_____

## STEP 4
## *Practical Lessons in Trust*

1. What are some areas in which you would like to trust God during this year? Be as specific as possible. List your ideas below.

*I would like to trust God—*

EXAMPLES
- for better grades in school.
- that I will find a part-time job.

Take a few minutes to pray about the areas you've just written down. Ask God to help you trust Him to meet those needs.

2. Now, write down some practical things you might be able to do that will help you learn to trust God more. In case you're really stuck, the examples may help you. (Even though this is a Bible study primarily about money, you'll want to learn to trust God in other areas as well, as the example demonstrates.)

*Practical things to do:*

EXAMPLES
- Pray daily for God's help to pay better attention in class.
- Set aside time each day to study.
- Ask a friend or family member to review my studies with me.
- Pray daily that I will find a job.
- Read the want ads daily for summer jobs.
- Check with friends about jobs and begin to develop leads.

# GOD IS MY BOSS

**In this lesson, you will . . .**
- Discover who you are ultimately working for in your job;
- Find out why and how that should affect your work habits.

## STEP 1
### *Boss for a Day*

Imagine that the next time you went to mow your neighbor's lawn, your neighbor announced, "I'm leaving for the rest of the day. I'd like you to meet the supervisor who will take my place while I'm gone—Jesus Christ."

Sure enough! Jesus Christ is there to see how well you do and oversee the yard work for the day.

**1.** How would you feel about Jesus being your boss for the day? _____

_____

_____

_____

2. What difference, if any, would Jesus being there make in how you acted and what you did?

_____

_____

_____

## STEP 2
## *"As Working for the Lord"*

"Whatever you do, work at it with all your heart, as working for the Lord, not for men" (Colossians 3:23).

1. What do you think it means to work "as working for the Lord"?

_____

_____

_____

2. Scripture gives us some principles (guidelines) to follow "as working for the Lord." Excellence, humility, and diligence are three godly principles each of us should work toward.
   • Look up the following sets of verses.
   • List which of the three principles (Excellence, Humility, or Diligence) you feel is best described in each set.
   • Then, unscramble the words in the definition of each principle.

*Principle 1:* _____

Proverbs 10:4; 13:4   Colossians 3:23
It means: kongriw rahd dna fitlefenicy

_____

*Principle 2:* _____

Numbers 18:29   1 Peter 4:11
It means: gonid het steb ylutiqa krow uyo anc os ogd si rhodone

_____

*Principle 3:* _____

Philippians 2:3,4   Matthew 20:25-28
It means: ton gringbag utoba lanetts, tub sugni meth ot phel sherot

_____

## STEP 3
## *Evaluating My Work Habits*

1. Even though diligence, excellence, and humility are principles we should all strive to live by on the job, at school, or at home, we sometimes live by just the opposite principles, and the final result will always be failure. Look up the verses listed below and write what you find described as a principle for failure—the opposite of God's principles for success.

| Bible Verses | Principles for Failure | God's Principles for Success |
|---|---|---|
| Proverbs 19:15 | _____ | Diligence |
| Proverbs 4:19 | _____ | Excellence |
| Proverbs 16:5 | _____ | Humility |

2. Now, mark an "X" in one of the three boxes under the four work locations on the chart to show which principles (either God's or the opposite) you work by most often. Be honest with yourself.

| PRINCIPLES I USUALLY FOLLOW | At home | On a job | In school | In church activities |
|---|---|---|---|---|
| DILIGENCE EXCELLENCE HUMILITY | | | | |
| A MIXTURE | | | | |
| LAZINESS EVIL MOTIVES PRIDE | | | | |

Which one of God's Principles for Success do you tend to follow most often?

_____

_____

Which one of the Principles for Failure do you tend to follow most often?

_____

_____

## STEP 4
### *On the Job*

You probably listed in the previous activity at least one area in which your work doesn't please God. But the good news is, God can help you change your life so you can live by the godly principles instead.

In what area would you most like to improve your actions—

- □ work?
- □ school?
- □ home?
- □ church?

Write a brief description of one improvement (be specific) you want to accomplish this month (or however long you feel you need). Set a realistic goal for this improvement.

EXAMPLE:

Improvement: I want to be more diligent in brushing the dog.

Goal: I'll brush him three times a week (Monday, Wednesday, Friday).

Improvement: _____

Goal: _____

_____

After you've written down your goal, sign your name. _____

Next, write your goal on an index card and post it in some visible place in your room at home. This will help you remember that you're serious about living by God's principles rather than the world's.

## More Questions for Thought

**1.** How can diligent, excellent and humble work glorify God?

_____

_____

**2.** How can God be glorified through one job you now do?

_____

_____

_____

**3.** Most people work primarily to make money. Why do you (or why don't you) think this is the best motivation for working?

_____

_____

_____

# TAKIN' CARE OF BUSINESS

**In this lesson, you will . . .**
- **Learn the difference between an owner and a steward;**
- **Discover that everything you have has been entrusted to you as a steward;**

- **Have an opportunity to commit yourself to being a faithful steward of God's business.**

## STEP 1
### *Whose Business Is It, Anyway?*

The apostle Paul helps us understand the role of a steward:

> Let a man regard us in this manner, as servants of Christ, and stewards of the mysteries of God. In this case, moreover, it is required of stewards that one be found trustworthy. . . . And what do you have that you did not receive? (1 Corinthians 4:1,2,7b).

That's a good question: "What do you have that you did not receive from someone else?"

1. In the left column on the next page, list things that you have aquired totally on your own. (Do not include anything that was given to you or that you obtained by trading something that was originally given to you.) In the right column, write how you obtained each item.

| I GOT— | I GOT IT BY— |
|---|---|
| | |
| | |
| | |

2. Now go back over your list and think a little more carefully about the history of each thing. Did you really earn or create anything all by yourself?

- How about the **time** required to earn or create it? Where did you get it? The Bible says God numbers our days and gives us the very breath of life.
- Where did you get the **intelligence, good looks, or strength** required? Didn't you inherit them as a gift from God and through your parents?
- Where did you get the **skills**? Didn't someone teach you?

It does not take long to see that everything we have is the result of what was given to us or what we traded that first was given to us. And ultimately the Source of all we have was God.

## STEP 2
## *A Parable of Three Stewards*

Read Matthew 25:14-30 carefully. Then answer these questions as best you can.

1. Why was each servant given a separate amount?

2. Did the owner expect each servant to earn the same amount?

3. How were the faithful servants rewarded?

4. What was done to the unfaithful servant?

5. The three servants were stewards. What is the difference between an owner and a steward?

_____

_____

_____

6. How does a good steward manage the property entrusted to him or her?

_____

_____

_____

7. How do we know if we are owners or stewards of our possessions? Explain your answer.

_____

_____

_____

8. What difference should this make in the way we use our money and possessions?

_____

_____

_____

## STEP 3
### _Windfall!_

1. Imagine that you've just been given $500, and now you have to decide what to do with it! Based on the following instructions, develop two possible spending plans.

### _The "Owner" Plan_

Imagine that $500 is all yours to use just as you please. How you spend it is no one else's business—not even God's. What kind of things might you do with your $500 windfall?

_____

_____

_____

_____

_____

_____

### The "Steward" Plan

God has just entrusted you with $500 of His money for you to manage for Him. Your mission is to use the $500 in ways which please God. What kind of things might you do with the money?

_____

_____

_____

_____

2. Now, look back over your two plans. Which one feels best to you? Why? (Be honest!)

_____

_____

_____

3. Which plan would produce the best results? Why?

_____

_____

_____

4. What are some differences you noticed between the owner's plan and the steward's plan?

_____

_____

_____

## STEP 4
## Quit-Claim Deed

Now that you have an understanding about the attitude of stewardship, it's a good idea to make a commitment to God to try to be the kind of steward He wants you to be.

1. Read the "Quit-Claim Deed" below.

---

**Quit-Claim Deed**

This deed is to serve notice that from this day on, I do not claim as my own anything I have—money, possessions, time, energy, or abilities. I recognize that these all belong to God, and that He has entrusted them to me to manage as He directs.

I, therefore, covenant with God to fulfill this stewardship to the best of my ability, investing, spending, or giving away these resources in ways which please God—not as if I owned them. I promise to study God's plan for managing these resources so I will know how He wishes them used.

Signed this _____ day of _____ , 19 _____

by _____

---

2. Pray silently for a few minutes and ask God to help you know if you're ready to sign this commitment. Of course, you don't have to sign it. You really should *not* sign it if you aren't convinced that this is the way God wants you to regard your things or if you aren't ready to do so.

3. After you've signed the quit-claim deed, ask God to show you a way to acknowledge His ownership this very week. You might try a prayer similar to this one:

> I know everything I have belongs to You and from this point on, I want to try to be a good steward of Your money. But, I know it's not going to be easy—I really need Your help, Lord.
>
> This week, show me in a specific way how You want me to use Your money so I can learn this important lesson on stewardship.
>
> I want to pray this according to Your will and in Jesus' name. Amen.

# THE SECRET OF CONTENTMENT

**In this lesson, you will...**

- Learn that it is human nature—but a mistake—to think that "more" will make us content;

- Discover what causes people to be discontented;
- Begin an exercise to learn contentment.

## STEP 1
### *How Much Would It Take?*

1. Each of us has thought some time or another about what a person "needs" to be satisfied. Write down what you think the "typical" family in your community needs to be content. Be specific.

_____

_____

_____

_____

_____

_____

2. Do you know any people who are content without some of these things?

☑ Yes.

☐ No, but I'm sure it's possible.

☐ No way! I only listed vital necessities!

3. Why might some people feel they need things that other people don't need?

_____

_____

## STEP 2
## *The Enemy of Contentment*

Read 1 Timothy 6:6-10. Then answer the following questions.

1. With what are we to be content? (verse 8)

_____

_____

2. What happens to people who want to get rich? (verse 9)

_____

_____

_____

3. What is the love of money? (verse 10)

_____

_____

_____

4. What have some people done because they were eager for money? (verse 10)

_____

_____

_____

5. How do you think Paul would answer someone who said, "If I only had more, then I would be content"? (See Philippians 4:11-13.)

_____

_____

## STEP 3
### *Diagnosing Discontent*

Have you ever felt any of the following symptoms of discontent? Put a check by the ones which sometimes describe you. You might want to add some of your own, too.

□ **Self-Pity**
When my friends have the latest styles and I don't, I feel deprived.

□ **Jealousy**
I can't feel my friends' joy when they have something I don't have. I know it's not their fault, but I think I resent them, anyway.

□ **Debt**
Sometimes I want to buy something, but I don't have the money, so I borrow it from my friends or family. Then I feel guilty when I don't pay it back.

□ **Get-Things-Quick Attitude**
I see things I want to have, and rather than save money, I think of the fastest way I can get them. Usually, I promise my parents that I'll do something I know I can't really live up to.

☑ **Other**
_____
_____

## STEP 4
### *Learning to Be Content*

1. Look up Philippians 4:6 and summarize it in your own words. What does it mean to you?

_____
_____
_____
_____
_____

2. Also look up Philippians 4:19. How does it relate to resolving dissatisfaction?

_____
_____
_____
_____
_____

Here's one way to tell if you're living by the secret of contentment: Whenever you need something you can't afford to buy, simply present your request to God and trust Him—either to provide it, or to withhold it, if that is better for you. If it hurts to pray that way, contentment is not yet a part of your life. You probably need to ask God to help you learn to trust Him more and to be content with what you have.

## STEP 5
### *Trust Project*

Think of something you believe you need. Think of something large enough that it would be difficult to get it from your own resources. Write down your request below. Ask God to provide it for you—if it's His will. Tell your parents what you think you need. If your parents say you should not have what you're praying for, be content with that as God's answer. If they do provide your need (or if God provides in another way), be content with your provision.

_____

_____

_____

# HEY, BIG SPENDER!

**In this lesson, you will . . .**
- **Learn how to recognize selfish spending patterns;**
- **Discover how to tell the difference between a need, a want, and a wish.**

## STEP 1
### *Shopping List*

Make a list of all the items you would like to have during this coming year. Be as specific as possible.

a Nice car of that Dart
another Gretsch Guitar
food and clothing
revHeat CD signayright in a box
brian Setzer New Swing CD
tickets to see Rev. live this year
Maximum Carnage the Sega Video game

## STEP 2
## *How to Spot a Big Spender*

1. The following statements describe a big spender. Check whichever ones you think might apply to you.

   ☑ He buys things that aren't very useful.
   ☑ She always shows off her things to everyone else.
   ☐ He makes a lot of phony friends by buying them things.
   ☐ She's constantly in the company of other big spenders.
   ☐ His closet is full of clothes he hardly ever wears.
   ☐ She can't resist a sale.
   ☑ His money "burns a hole in his pocket."

2. What are some other statements that would describe a big spender?

   _all begs _____
   _____
   _____

## STEP 3
## *Rags, Riches, or. . .?*

1. In Proverbs 30:8, what standard of living did the author want? (Circle the correct answer.)

   a. poverty
   b. riches
   ⓒ other (describe) _He wanted _____

2. Where does selfish spending lead?
   Proverbs 21:17 _to poverty _____
   Ecclesiastes 2:10,11 _____
   Luke 8:14 _____

3. What should the Christian do instead of satisfying his or her every appetite, whim, and desire? (Luke 9:23.)

   _____
   _____

4. Consider this statement: "God promises to supply every need, not every desire. To satisfy our every whim and desire moves us out of God's will." Do you agree or disagree? (Explain your answer.)

   _yes _____
   _____
   _____

**STEP 4**
## Needs, Wants, and Wishes

1. Thinking of your own family, fill in the following chart as best you can. For instance, in the line marked "Transportation," you might fill in "shoes" as your need, "bicycle" as your want, but "motor scooter" as your desire. Or for the "Food" row you might list "Beans and rice" as your need, "Steak" as your want, and "Eat out often" as your desire.

**Needs:** Food, clothes, a place to live, health care, a job, etc.
**Wants:** Comforts, conveniences, things a little nicer than you have to have.
**Wishes:** Luxuries, items you can easily get along without.

| | NEEDS | WANTS | WISHES |
|---|---|---|---|
| **TRANSPORTATION** | | | |
| **FOOD** | | | |
| **CLOTHES** | | | |
| **HOUSING** | | | |
| **RECREATION** | | | |

2.  Now go back to your shopping list (step 1), and next to each item listed, put an "N" if it's a need, a "W" if it's a want, or a "?" if it's a wish.

3.  What did your list have the most of—needs, wants, or wishes?

    _Wishes_

4.  Do you think the Lord is pleased with your list?

    _Sure_

5.  If not, what can you do to change it?

    _I can't_

## STEP 5
### *Saying No to Selfish Spending*

1.  How can you use the "Needs-Wants-Wishes" technique as a tool to avoid selfish spending?

    _To help protect from it_

2.  What do you think are some rewards of avoiding selfish spending?

    _you nothing to be Discontent_

3.  What guidelines should a Christian use to determine his or her lifestyle? (Consider some of the Bible verses we have been studying in this course.)

    _the Bible_

# DEBT ROW

**In this lesson, you will . . .**
- Discover some of the problems of borrowing money;
- Learn how God sometimes uses the availability of money to guide us (and how borrowing can confuse His guidance);
- Develop some guidelines for borrowing.

## STEP 1
### *To Borrow or Not to Borrow*

Imagine that your friend Jim asks you for advice concerning this problem:

> I'm trying to decide what stereo to buy. My cousin is willing to sell me his old stereo for $40. It's pretty good, and I've saved enough to pay cash for it. But I can get a nicer, new one for $325. My parents will loan me the money at low interest and I can pay it off over the next year. What do you think I should do?

**1.** What would be the advantages of buying the $325 system?

_____

_____

_____

_____

**2.** What would be the advantages of buying the $40 stereo?

_____

_____

_____

**3.** What would be your final advice to Jim? Give your reasons.

_____

_____

_____

## STEP 2
## *The Range of God's Will*

A major part of taking out a loan is your promise to pay it back in the future. But that promise means you aren't free to do other things with your future money or the time required to earn it. This is why debt can be a bondage. You are bound to do what you promise.

**1.** Read James 4:13-17, and then answer the following questions:

  **a.** What's wrong with making promises about what you will do in the future (like paying back a loan)?

  _____

  _____

  **b.** What does it mean to say, "If the Lord wills, we shall...do this or that"?

  _____

  _____

  **c.** In terms of this passage, how would saving for something you want differ from borrowing to buy it?

  _____

  _____

**2.** Does God ever allow borrowing?

  **a.** Look up Matthew 5:42. What does it tell us to do?

  _____

  _____

  **b.** Would God ask us to help someone do something that was basically wrong?

  _____

  **c.** Then what does this verse tell us about whether borrowing is always wrong?

  _____

**3.** Does God suggest that borrowing is a desirable thing? How does God describe debt in Proverbs 22:7?

_____

_____

---

**4.** According to Deuteronomy 15:4-6, those who follow God's plan will not need to
_____ but will be able to _____
_____
_____

**5.** To summarize God's counsel regarding borrowing, how would you describe what is Good, Better and Best?—

a. Good—Psalm 37:21 gives God's absolute minimum standard for borrowing:
_____
_____

b. Better—Romans 13:8 says it is better to: _____
_____

c. Best—Luke 6:34, 35 says it is best to be able to: _____
_____

## STEP 3
## *God's Traffic Light*

"One year, my wife and I planned to go on vacation, but we weren't able to save the money. Instead of using our credit cards, we decided we'd better just stay home. Then, a few months later, some friends called. They had rented a houseboat for a week and asked us to come along as their guests. So by waiting, we ended up having a better vacation which cost us hardly anything."—*Larry Burkett*

Here are some questions to think about concerning ways God uses money in the lives of Christians:

**1.** Has money ever been provided or withheld so you or your family felt God was guiding in a decision? In what ways?

_____
_____

**2.** How could borrowing make it harder to know God's direction in a decision?

_____
_____

**3.** How could borrowing demonstrate a lack of trust in God's promise to provide?

_____

_____

_____

**4.** How could borrowing reveal a lack of contentment?

_____

_____

_____

## STEP 4
## *Guidelines for Borrowers*

The following case study examples are for you to think about. Analyze the case study assigned to you for a few minutes. Then write in the space below it the suggestions you have, as well as the scriptural principle you used to formulate your suggestions.

These three guidelines (as well as other scriptural principles you've learned) will help you as you analyze the case studies.

**1. Pay it back.** Never borrow money you can't pay back on time. Only the wicked do that (Psalm 37:21).

**2. Give God a chance to provide.** God may want to give you something debt-free! But, if you impatiently buy it on credit, you may short-circuit God's better plan (Philippians 4:6).

**3. Keep it small, if at all!** While God's Word doesn't rule out borrowing, it discourages it. Borrow sparingly, if at all (Philippians 4:19).

## Case Study One

Return to the example of your friend Jim as he is trying to decide between two stereo systems—a used one he can pay $40 cash for, and a nicer, new one for $325, on which he would have to make payments over the next year.

Scriptural principle or guideline: _____

Your suggestions: _____

_____

## Case Study Two

Sue wants to go to her church summer camp. But it is rather expensive and is scheduled for the first week of summer vacation. There won't be time for her to earn the money before camp. Should she try to find someone who will loan her the camp fee, hoping to pay it back after camp with a summer job? She believes God wants her to go to camp, but she wants to be careful not to ignore God's leadership and timing by borrowing.

Scriptural principle or guideline: _____

_____

Your suggestions: _____

_____

_____

## Case Study Three

Frank is in the eighth grade and wants to trade in his old ten-speed for a new fifteen-speed mountain bike. To get the mountain bike Frank would have to (1) use all his savings as a down payment, (2) take out a $300 loan, (3) cut back on his spending in other areas to make the payments, and (4) increase his after-school work from eight to twelve hours each week.

Scriptural principle or guideline: _____

_____

Your suggestions: _____

_____

_____

## Case Study Four

The junior high youth group has taken on the job of painting the church fellowship hall as a project. They raised most of the money and have started the work. But before they finished, they ran out of money. They need $100 for more paint to finish the job. Someone suggests asking the church board to lend them the money, which they will pay off within the year.

Scriptural principle or guideline: _____

_____

Your suggestions: _____

_____

_____

---

## STEP 5
### *Get Out and Stay Out!*

Listed below are four practical steps to getting out of debt and staying out. After discussing these steps for a few minutes with others in your class, put the steps in what you believe is the correct order.

- Contact creditors (Proverbs 3:27).
- Develop a plan to pay back debts (Psalm 37:21).
- Develop a budget to control future spending (Proverbs 6:6-8).
- Stop borrowing and spending—Cut up all credit cards (Proverbs 21:17).

1. _____
2. _____
3. _____
4. _____

Now write down the reasons you chose the order you did.

_____
_____
_____
_____
_____
_____
_____
_____

# NOW, HONESTLY!

**In this lesson, you will . . .**
- Discover why God allows our honesty to be tested;
- Learn how important complete honesty is;
- Have an opportunity to determine the honest response in sample situations;
- Find out how to make it right if you have been dishonest in the past.

## STEP 1
### *It's Tempting*

**1. "The Slow Leak"**

Your old bike still looks okay, but both tires have slow leaks. It wouldn't take much to fix them—a few bucks for new tubes—but why put money into it when you want to sell it and get a new one?

You advertised in the paper for $60, but only one person has responded. He looks it over and says that he'll give you $50.

Actually, even though you honestly think the bike is worth $60 (even with the leaky tires) you could live with $50. It will just give you enough—along with what you have already saved—to get that new trail bike you've wanted.

But then, just before your potential buyer hands you his money, he asks, "Are you sure everything is in good shape on this bike?"

**What would you be tempted to say?**

_____

_____

**2.** **"Pretty Good Deal"**

You've been trying to get to K-Mart for three days to get in on a sale of blank tapes for your cassette player. Finally you make it.

The clerk rings it up and—shock: she is charging you full price!

"But this is supposed to be on sale."

"Oh, sorry, that sale ended yesterday. $11.79."

You stand there trying to decide if you can afford it, until someone in the line behind you mumbles, "What's the hold-up?" So you fork over a twenty.

But when the clerk hands you back the change, it includes a ten dollar bill along with the ones and coins. You walk away trying to calculate whether it was really a mistake.

Yes, yes. It should have been a five with those ones. That means you did get the tapes for almost half price. Pretty good deal after all...or was it?

**What would you be tempted to do?**

_____

_____

**3.** Why are such temptations attractive to us?

_____

_____

_____

**4.** What is the problem with giving in to those temptations?

_____

_____

_____

# STEP 2
## *Why Are We Tested?*

**1.** Summarize what Jesus said in Luke 16:10 about dealing with little problems.

_____

_____

_____

**2.** Why is this true?

_____

_____

_____

**3.** Who fails when the stakes are high?

_____

_____

_____

_____

**STEP 3**
## Words to the Wise

Fill in the truth each verse gives about being honest.

Truth One—Proverbs 20:17

_____

_____

_____

Truth Two—Proverbs 20:23

_____

_____

_____

Truth Three—Proverbs 28:6

_____

_____

_____

Truth Four—Luke 16:10

_____

_____

_____

Truth Five—Romans 13:6,7

_____

_____

_____

**STEP 4**
## Making It Right

To enjoy financial freedom, you must have a clear conscience. This means if you have been dishonest or unfair with someone, you must make it right. You'll never experience financial freedom any other way.

1. Read Proverbs 28:13 and think about it for a few minutes. Then write out the meaning of the verse using the fewest words possible.

   _____

   _____

2. How did Zacchaeus make things right with those he had cheated? (Use Luke 19:8 for help.)

   _____

   _____

## STEP 5
## *Guide for Prayer*

The easiest way to make things right is to start with prayer. Remember, you're not alone! God will help you know what to say when you approach someone to ask forgiveness. Use the following guide to begin the process of making things right.

- Ask God to bring to your mind anyone you have treated dishonestly or unfairly.
- Now ask Him to show you how to make things right.
- Thank Him for showing you this step toward financial freedom.
- Finally, ask Him for courage to follow through.

# YOU CAN'T TAKE IT WITH YOU

**In this lesson, you will...**
- **Discover the difference between saving and hoarding;**
- **Find out what a Christian should do about saving;**
- **Develop a personal savings plan.**

## STEP 1
### *A Penny Saved*

Why do you think people save money? Include both good and bad reasons in your answers. Be as specific as possible. Write your answers in the spaces provided in the coins below.

**STEP 2**

## *How Much Is Enough?*

How much should a Christian save? Answer the following questions and find out what God has to say about it.

1. Read Luke 12:16-21.
   a. Why did God confront the rich man? _____
   _____
   _____

   b. Why did the rich man hoard? _____
   _____
   _____

   c. Who else will share this rich man's fate? _____
   _____
   _____

2. What is the danger of riches? (See Proverbs 30:7-9.)
   _____
   _____
   _____

3. Read Matthew 6:19,20.
   a. What do you think these verses mean? _____
   _____
   _____

   b. In this passage, what do you think it means to lay up treasures in heaven? (See also 1 Timothy 6:18, 19.)
   _____
   _____
   _____

4. Should a Christian save at all?
   a. Read Proverbs 6:6-11. Why is the ant praised? _____
   _____
   _____
   _____

   b. Look up Proverbs 21:20. What is the difference between the wise and the foolish man?
   _____
   _____
   _____
   _____

## STEP 3
## *Hoarding Versus Saving*

The following four attitudes reveal hoarding.

**Fear** about what might happen in the future (Matthew 6:25-31).

**Selfish** unwillingness to share from savings when others have needs (1 John 3:17).

**False contentment** without God because of riches (Proverbs 30:8,9).

**"Collecting Fever"**—Saving just to pile up money for no particular, legitimate reason (Ecclesiastes 4:7,8).

1. Choose one of these attitudes and write in your own words how this attitude could possibly happen in your own life.

   Attitude: _____

   _____

   _____

2. Now write down some ideas on how you could avoid this wrong attitude.

   _____

   _____

   _____

3. Some questions for thought:
   a. What do you think the difference is between wise saving and hoarding?

   _____

   _____

   _____

   _____

   b. What are some good things to save money for?

   _____

   _____

   _____

   _____

## STEP 4
## *Your Savings Plan*

1. Look up the following verses to find the two main problems with hoarding.
   a. Matthew 6:19 _____

   _____

   _____

b. Matthew 6:21 (also see Luke 18:24) _____

_____

Even though "you can't take it with you" when you die, the Bible instructs us to do this by storing up treasure in heaven. But how can that be done?

**2.** What should the person do who has been hoarding (Luke 18:22)?

_____

_____

**3.** What will happen to those who quietly help the needy (Matthew 6:3,4)?

_____

_____

**4.** What will be the reward of faithful servants (Matthew 25:21)?

_____

_____

You should be "saving" in your heavenly bank throughout your life. Ask God to help you develop a well-balanced savings plan.

---

### MY SAVINGS PLAN

**PART ONE**
*Stores in the House of the Wise*

**1.** What should I be saving toward? _____

_____

_____

**2.** How much do I want to set aside for this each week or month? _____

_____

Remember: Better to save and pay cash than to make loan payments.

**PART TWO**
*Treasures in Heaven*

What is my plan for laying up treasures in heaven?

_____

_____

_____

"Do not store up for yourselves treasures on earth....But store up for yourselves treasures in heaven" (Matthew 6:19,20).

---

# SHARING GOD'S WAY— THE TITHE

**In this lesson, you will . . .**
- Learn when and why tithing began;
- Explore whether it is a practice that should be followed by Christians today;
- Consider some difficult situations concerning whether or not someone should tithe.

## STEP 1
### *Is Tithing for Today?*

*Tithe = one tenth*

*Tithing = giving one tenth of your income*

Answer these questions to find out what the Bible says about tithing.

1.  The tithe did not begin with the Jewish Law. Over 400 years before God gave Moses the Ten Commandments, people of faith tithed. Look up Genesis 14:18-20. Why did Abraham (Abram) tithe to Melchizedek?

_____

_____

2. Even though Christ condemned legalism, He still told us to obey the Bible. Read Matthew 23:23. Mark the box in front of the answer you believe is what Christ said when He rebuked the Pharisees for hypocrisy:
   - □ a. Forget the tithe and concentrate on justice, mercy, and faithfulness.
   - □ b. Practice justice, mercy, and faithfulness without neglecting the tithe.
   - □ c. Do whatever seems best because you should no longer be under the Law.

3. Turn to Malachi 3:8 (the last book of the Old Testament). What does God say avoiding the tithe is like?

   _____

   _____

## STEP 2
## *Why Tithe, Anyway?*

1. Have you ever wondered why God set up a clear-cut minimum standard for giving? Why wouldn't He just encourage everyone to give whatever they wanted to give? In the space below, write down some reasons you think God might have set up the practice of tithing.

   _____

   _____

   _____

   _____

2. Mark the box in front of the statement that you think is the main purpose of the tithe.

   - □ a. Tithing proves Christians believe and obey the Old Testament Law.
   - □ b. Giving a tithe is an evidence of God's ownership of all our resources.
   - □ c. The practice of tithing makes sure poor people are taken care of.

## STEP 3
## *What to Do?*

Read the following situations. Then write down what you think the correct response to the issue of tithing should be.

1. Joe has a paper route each evening. His family is rather poor, and Joe must use all his own earnings for clothes, school lunches, school supplies, and bus money. After he pays all those expenses, he has very little for spending money. What

should he do about giving money to the Lord's work? _____

_____

_____

2. Jane volunteered to spend her summer helping to lead neighborhood Bible clubs for younger children. She doesn't get paid with regular wages, but the church gives her a $25 per week gratuity (a "gift" of appreciation for her service). Should she tithe it? The money was already "tithed" when people gave to the church in the first place; so it's not really income, or is it? Explain your answer.

_____

_____

_____

3. Gary makes $10 every Saturday doing yard work for a neighbor. His take-home pay is $40.00 a month. He gives $4.00 to his church every month. In October his grandparents sent him $15.00 for his birthday. He dropped $1.50 in the church missionary fund. At Christmas, the needs of homeless children were made known to Gary in his Sunday school class. Gary felt good that he had already given his tithe and did not need to give anymore. What do you think of Gary's approach?

_____

_____

_____

## STEP 4
## *Wrapping Up*

Consider praying the following prayer of commitment concerning your money.

Dear Lord,
I know that tithing really involves my letting
You be the Owner over all my things.
So, Lord, help me to have a healthy attitude toward giving.
I want to be a cheerful giver to Your work.
In Jesus' name, Amen.

# SHARING FROM OBEDIENCE, ABUNDANCE, AND SACRIFICE

**In this lesson, you will . . .**
- Discover the differences between giving from obedience, abundance, and sacrifice;
- Find out why we can give sacrificially

and still not suffer deprivation of our basic necessities;
- Work out a specific giving plan for yourself.

## STEP 1
### *Sharing from Obedience*

Read Matthew 25:31-40. After you've thought about this passage for a few minutes, write down in your own words what you think the passage means.

_____

_____

_____

_____

_____

_____

## STEP 2
## *Sharing from Abundance*

1. Read 2 Corinthians 8:13-15. What do you think Paul was talking about when he used the word, "equality"?

_____

_____

_____

_____

_____

You may never have thought of your income as providing you with an abundance of money. However, anything you have extra beyond what you really need qualifies as "abundance."

2. Write out a few practical ways you could give out of your abundance—your extra, discretionary funds.

_____

_____

_____

_____

## STEP 3
## *Sharing from Sacrifice*

In Luke 21:1-4 Jesus commented on a poor widow who gave two coins in the temple. This is an example of sacrificial giving. Explain why the widow's gift pleased Christ more than the larger gifts from the rich.

_____

_____

_____

_____

Remember: "Do not forget to do good and to share with others, for with such sacrifices God is pleased" (Hebrews 13:16).

## STEP 4
## *My Sharing Plan*

To review one more time, giving to God includes:

- **The tithe**—a testimony to God's ownership.
- **Obedience**—helping meet the obvious needs around us.
- **Abundance**—helping others from our abundance (savings, earnings, etc.).
- **Sacrifice**—giving up our needs for others.

Now that you understand giving a little better, try working out a specific plan to help you become a better steward. The following chart might help:

---

My estimated income for the month: $ _____

My tithe: $_____

For those who are committed to giving beyond the tithe, the following guidelines should help:

**Obedience:**
To help meet the needs of people in greatest need,
I will set aside $_____ of my income for sharing.

**Abundance:**
If I receive unexpected income,
I will set aside _____ percent of that surplus for sharing.

I will use the rest of my surplus for _____
_____

**Sacrifice:**
In order to share with others who have less,
I am willing to do without the following items in my usual monthly budget:
_____
_____
_____

---

# WHO DESERVES HELP?

**In this lesson, you will . . .**
- **Learn whom we are to help financially;**
- **Discover how helping people in need is**

really giving to God;
- **Do a skit on familiar excuses for not helping.**

## STEP 1
### *Whom the Bible Says to Help*

**1.** Look up the following Scriptures and match them to the functions on the right. You will discover several ways that we can give to God by meeting various needs.

| | |
|---|---|
| 1. Malachi 3:10a | A. Support for ministers. |
| 2. 1 Timothy 5:17,18 | B. Helping needy relatives. |
| 3. 2 Corinthians 8:1-5 | C. Supporting missionaries. |
| 4. 1 Timothy 5:8 | D. Funding church programs. |
| 5. Matthew 19:21 | E. Sharing with Christians. |
| 6. Philippians 4:15-17 | F. Giving to the poor. |

**2.** Now list some people you know who fall into one of these six groups. Then check those to whom you would like to consider giving.

Ministers: _____

_____

Needy Relatives: _____

_____

Missionaries: _____

_____

Church Programs: _____

_____

Christians: _____

_____

The Poor: _____

_____

**3.** Look up 2 Thessalonians 3:10 and answer the following questions:

- Are there some people you don't need to help when they ask?
  Who? _____

  _____

  _____

- What does this verse imply about people who can't work?

  _____

  _____

  _____

## STEP 2
## *Sharing with Your Family*

Are there ways you can give to your family and relatives? Remember, giving doesn't always have to involve money. Below, write down a family member or relative you'd like to help and how you can go about helping.

I'd like to help— _____

_____

My plan for helping— _____

_____

_____

_____

_____

## STEP 3
### *Sharing with the Body of Christ*

1. Look up 1 John 3:17,18. What does God conclude if we have a surplus and find a fellow Christian in need, but don't help him or her?

_____

_____

_____

_____

_____

_____

2. Can you think of a time when you could have helped to meet a need, but didn't? Describe what happened. (Remember, needs aren't always financial and giving money isn't the only way to help.)

_____

_____

_____

_____

How did you feel? _____

_____

3. What about a time when you did meet a need? Describe it.

_____

_____

_____

How did you feel then? _____

_____

**STEP 4**
## *Hey, Mister Christian!*

Read the following skit, "Hey, Mr. Christian!"

**Hey, Mister Christian!**

## *SCENE I*

**Poor Mother:** I need a little help. A friend of mine said I should talk to you. You see, I'm having a tough time getting enough food for my family this week, and I'm worried about the baby because he hasn't had anything to eat for. . .

**Mr. Christian:** Oh, I'm sorry to hear that. And your friend was right. You'll always find a Christian ready to help. You know, years ago, our church had a fund to help people like you. It was a good thing, too. But when we started the new building. . .well, we needed all the money for it, so we kind of got out of the food business.

## *SCENE II*

**Teenager:** Hey, man. A couple friends of mine are coming through town next week and need a place to stay. Would you know of any place? What's that? Oh, they don't live any place in particular—just kind of travel around. Hitchhike, you know. Sleep outside a lot.

**Mr. Christian:** Well, I'd sure like to help, but we don't have an extra bed. They'd have to sleep on the floor, and I'd hate to put them out like that. Maybe someone else would be more set up to handle them.

## *SCENE III*

**Unemployed Worker:** I'm kind of ashamed to ask, but my family's clothes are pretty well shot; the girl's even embarrassed to go to school, and. . .well, I heard that maybe you would be able to help us out.

**Mr. Christian:** I'll tell you, if I had the money I'd go down and buy clothes for you right now. But I'm planning to give all my extra money to the big missionary offering Sunday—and you know how important that is.

**Unemployed Worker:** Well, Mr. Christian, my little girl is in the hospital, and she's really lonely, even depressed. Do you suppose. . .

**Mr. Christian:** Sure! Our pastor is out of town for a couple days, but just as soon as he gets back, I'll give him a call. I'm sure he'd be glad to drop by. The church will probably even send some flowers.

**Unemployed Worker:** And, Mr. Christian, my son got picked up by the police last week, and it looks like he may have a long stay ahead in jail. He's really on a bad guilt trip. He could probably use a friend. Do you know of. . .

**Mr. Christian:** Is he interested in becoming a Christian? That's what he really needs, you know. Any time he wants to pray, our pastor will be ready and waiting. Say, by the way, would you like to come to church with me Sunday? Not interested? From what you said at first, I thought maybe you really wanted help. Guess I was wrong, huh?

**Narrator:**

I was hungry, and you gave me nothing to eat,

I was thirsty, and you gave me nothing to drink,

I was a stranger, and you did not invite me in,

I needed clothes and you did not clothe me,

I was sick

And in prison and you did not look after me.

Whatever you did not do for one of the least of these,

You did not do for me.

(Words of Jesus—Matthew 25:42-45)

(Adapted from *CONQUEST,* 1975, Nazarene Publishing House, Kansas City, Missouri. Used by permission.)

## STEP 5
## *You Did It to Me!*

Read Matthew 25:34-46. Think about the message of the passage.

1. What are some reasons God might want us to help the needy?

_____

_____

_____

_____

_____

_____

_____

_____

2. What are the consequences if we don't help the needy?

_____

_____

_____

_____

**Optional Activity:** Choose one of the phrases listed below and illustrate it creatively. You might want to make a collage from magazine clippings, write a poem, sketch a picture, make a banner or something else.

a. "I was hungry, and you gave me something to eat."
b. "I was a stranger, and you invited me in."
c. "I was naked, and you clothed me."
d. "I was sick, and you visited me."
e. "I was in prison, and you came to me."

Remember: "A generous man will himself be blessed, for he shares his food with the poor" (Proverbs 22:9).

## Sometimes "No" Is Okay

When trying to decide which fund-raising appeals are deserving of help, ask these questions of some Christian leaders you respect:

- Is the organization communicating a message true to the Scriptures?
- Are people responding positively?
- Is the organization seeking and accomplishing worthy goals?
- Are the lives of the leaders consistent with scriptural principles?
- Is the organization training and equipping people to expand its work?
- Is there a standard of excellence along with freedom from waste?
- What do other Christian organizations say about it?

# ON TO FREEDOM!

**In this lesson, you will . . .**
- Review the things that have meant the most to you in this course, and identify what things you still want to work on in terms of being a good steward;
- Discover "where your money goes" each

month; then make a plan where you would like it to go, based on things you have learned in this course;
- Be able to participate in a group covenant of stewardship.

## STEP 1
## *The Growing Edge*

**1.** What is one important concept you've learned in this course?

_____

_____

_____

_____

_____

2. What is one way you are already using something you learned in this study?

_____

_____

_____

_____

3. What would you like to be doing that you learned in this course, but haven't started putting into practice yet?

_____

_____

_____

_____

## STEP 2
## *Your Next Step*

1. Choose one of the following "Ten Steps to Financial Freedom."

**Ten Steps to Financial Freedom**

- ☐ 1. Acknowledge that God owns everything you have.
- ☐ 2. Determine to manage God's resources by His desires, not yours.
- ☐ 3. Trust God, not yourself, to meet your needs.
- ☑ 4. Be content with what God provides you.
- ☐ 5. Work as though God is your boss; He is.
- ☐ 6. Don't indulge your whims and desires.
- ☐ 7. Get out of debt and stay out.
- ☐ 8. Always be fair and honest.
- ☐ 9. Save, but don't hoard.
- ☐ 10. Give as generously as God directs.

2. Write a paragraph that either explains why the step you chose is important, or that gives an example of that step being put into practice.

_____

_____

_____

_____

_____

_____

_____

_____

**3.** Of the ten steps, which one needs to be your next step toward financial freedom?

_____

**4.** If you obey this principle, how will it change the way you live?

_____

_____

_____

_____

_____

_____

## STEP 3
### *Where the Money Goes*

Think through your personal "income" and "outgo."

• Do you know where your money goes?

• Are you frustrated because the money somehow seems to slip through your fingers?

• Is your money getting used in the best possible way?

### *A. How It's Been*

On the next page, estimate as best you can what your sources and amount of income are, and then how it gets spent in a typical month. Some money may come from your parents for you to use on specific items. For example, many parents provide money for lunches, bus fare, supplies, clothes, etc. List any money of that type under both Income (Designated) and Spending.

## Monthly Income

| Source | Amount |
|---|---|
| Allowance _____ | _____ |
| Baby-sitting _____ | _____ |
| Part-time job _____ | _____ |
| Designated for specific expenses _____ | _____ |
| Total | _____ |

## Monthly Spending

| What for | Amount |
|---|---|
| Giving, tithe _____ | _____ |
| _____ | _____ |
| Saving for _____ | _____ |
| _____ | _____ |
| School: bus fare, lunch, supplies _____ | _____ |
| _____ | _____ |
| Debts to pay back _____ | _____ |
| _____ | _____ |
| Snacks, candy, pizza _____ | _____ |
| _____ | _____ |
| Movies, videos, magazines _____ | _____ |
| _____ | _____ |
| Activities _____ | _____ |
| _____ | _____ |
| Transportation (bicycle, bus, etc.) _____ | _____ |
| _____ | _____ |
| Hobbies _____ | _____ |
| _____ | _____ |
| Clothes _____ | _____ |
| _____ | _____ |
| Gifts   (friends) _____ | _____ |
|       (family) _____ | _____ |
| Other _____ | _____ |
| _____ | _____ |
| _____ | _____ |
| Total | _____ |

## B. A New Plan

Now make a new plan based on what you have learned in this course. Are there additional ways you can earn the money you need? What would you like to change about your spending?

**Monthly Income**

| Source | Amount |
|---|---|
| Allowance _____ | _____ |
| Baby-sitting _____ | _____ |
| Part-time job _____ | _____ |
| Designated for specific expenses _____ | _____ |
| Total | _____ |

**Monthly Spending**

| What for | Amount |
|---|---|
| Giving, tithe _____ | _____ |
| Saving for _____ | _____ |
| School: bus fare, lunch, supplies _____ | _____ |
| Debts to pay back _____ | _____ |
| Snacks, candy, pizza _____ | _____ |
| Movies, videos, magazines _____ | _____ |
| Activities _____ | _____ |
| Transportation (bicycle, bus, etc.) _____ | _____ |
| Hobbies _____ | _____ |
| Clothes _____ | _____ |
| Gifts  (friends) _____ | _____ |
| (family) _____ | _____ |
| Other _____ | _____ |
| Total | _____ |

## STEP 4
## *My Covenant of Stewardship*

This section summarizes the primary concepts of this course in the form of a covenant—a solemn pledge to obey God in managing His resources.

Write a description of one way you can respond to at least one of the statements from God's Word. See the two Sample Responses.

**God's Word:** "The earth is the Lord's, and everything in it, the world, and all who live in it" (Psalm 24:1).

**Sample Response:** Everything we have, Father, belongs to You.

**God's Word:** "Wealth and honor come from you; you are the ruler of all things. In your hands are strength and power to exalt and give strength to all" (1 Chronicles 29:12).

**Sample Response:** We are not owners, but managers of Your creation.

**God's Word:** "Honor the Lord from your wealth, with the firstfruits of all your crops" (Proverbs 3:9).

**Response:** _____

_____

**God's Word:** "Trust in the Lord with all your heart and lean not on your own understanding; in all your ways acknowledge him, and he will make your paths straight" (Proverbs 3:5, 6).

**Response:** _____

_____

**God's Word:** "But seek first his kingdom and his righteousness, and all these things will be given to you as well" (Matthew 6:33).

**Response:** _____

_____

_____

**God's Word:** "I know what it is to be in need, and I know what it is to have plenty. I have learned the secret of being content in any and every situation, whether well fed or hungry, whether living in plenty or in want" (Philippians 4:12).

**Response:** _____

_____

**God's Word:** "If anyone would come after Me, he must deny himself, and take up his cross daily, and follow Me" (Luke 9:23).

**Response:** _____

_____

**God's Word:** "Owe nothing to anyone except to love one another" (Romans 13:8, NASB).

**Response:** _____

_____

**God's Word:** "Whatever you do, work at it with all your heart, as working for the Lord, not for men" (Colossians 3:23).

**Response:** _____

_____

**God's Word:** "Better to be poor and honest than rich and dishonest" (Proverbs 28:6, TEV).

**Response:** _____

_____

**God's Word:** "Do not store up for yourselves treasures upon earth, where moth and rust destroy, and where thieves break in and steal, but store up for yourselves treasures in heaven" (Matthew 6:19,20).

**Response:** _____

_____

**God's Word:** "The man with two tunics should share with him who has none; and the one who has food should do the same" (Luke 3:11).

**Response:** _____

_____

**Response:** In all these ways we desire to be faithful, so that when we stand before You to give account for our stewardship, we can hear You say. . .

**God's Word:** "Well done, good and faithful servant! You have been faithful with a few things; I will put you in charge of many things. Come and share your master's happiness!" (Matthew 25:23).